Explanation of quarter sheet 91 S. W. of the one-inch geological survey map of England and Wales, illustrating the geology of the country around Blackpool, Poulton, and Fleetwood

Charles Eugene De Rance

MEMOIRS OF THE GEOLOGICAL SURVEY

OF

ENGLAND AND WALES.

EXPLANATION OF QUARTER SHEET 91 S.W. OF THE ONE-INCH GEOLOGICAL SURVEY MAP OF ENGLAND AND WALES,

ILLUSTRATING

THE GEOLOGY

OF

THE COUNTRY AROUND BLACKPOOL, POULTON, AND FLEETWOOD.

BY

C. E. DE RANCE, F.G.S.

PUBLISHED BY ORDER OF THE LORDS COMMISSIONERS OF HER MAJESTY'S TREASURY.

LONDON

PRINTED FOR HER MAJESTY'S STATIONERY OFFICE.

PUBLISHED BY

LONGMANS, GREEN, & Co.

AND BY

EDWARD STANFORD, 6, CHARING CROSS, S.W.

1875.

[*Price Sixpence.*]

NOTICE.

The SESSION of the ROYAL SCHOOL OF MINES and of SCIENCE applied to the ARTS commences early in October in each year, during which the following Courses of Lectures are delivered :—

Chemistry, with special reference to its applications in the Arts and Manufactures - - - } E. Frankland, F.R.S.

General Natural History - - T. H. Huxley, LL.D., F.R.S.

Physics - - - - F. Guthrie, F.R.S.

Applied Mechanics - - T. M. Goodeve, M.A.

Metallurgy - - - John Percy, M.D., F.R.S.

Geology - - - - A. C. Ramsay, LL.D., F.R.S.

Mining and Mineralogy - W. W. Smyth, M.A., F.R.S., (*Chairman*).

Mechanical Drawing - - J. H. Edgar, M.A.

The Chemical Laboratory (at South Kensington), under the direction of Dr. Frankland, and the Metallurgical Laboratory (in Jermyn Street), under the direction of Dr. Percy, are open for the instruction of Students.

N.B.—By order of the Lords Commissioners of the Privy Council on Education the Lectures on Chemistry Natural History, Physics, and Applied Mechanics are delivered at the Science Schools, South Kensington.

A Prospectus and Information may be obtained on application to

TRENHAM REEKS, *Registrar*.

Jermyn Street, London, S.W.

MEMOIRS OF THE GEOLOGICAL SURVEY

OF

ENGLAND AND WALES.

EXPLANATION OF QUARTER SHEET 91 S.W. OF THE ONE-INCH GEOLOGICAL SURVEY MAP OF ENGLAND AND WALES,

ILLUSTRATING

THE GEOLOGY

OF

THE COUNTRY AROUND BLACKPOOL, POULTON, AND FLEETWOOD.

BY

C. E. DE RANCE, F.G.S.

PUBLISHED BY ORDER OF THE LORDS COMMISSIONERS OF HER MAJESTY'S TREASURY

LONDON·

PRINTED FOR HER MAJESTY'S STATIONERY OFFICE

PUBLISHED BY

LONGMANS, GREEN, & Co.

AND BY

EDWARD STANFORD, 6, CHARING CROSS, S.W.

1875.

[*Price Sixpence.*]

TABLE OF CONTENTS.

GEOLOGY

OF

THE COUNTRY AROUND BLACKPOOL, POULTON, AND FLEETWOOD.

THE district comprised within this quarter-sheet, may be physically divided into three areas. The central and largest consists of glacial drifts, rising to an elevation of 40 to 130 feet above the sea, forming the western prolongation of the plain of Boulder Clay and sands upon which the towns of Preston and Kirkham are built, and which resting upon an ancient "plane of marine denudation," composed of various rocks, stretches away from Grit hills of Chipping and Longridge, west-ward towards and to the present sea-margin, at Blackpool and Bispham, where it abruptly terminates in a line of cliffs, from 50 to 75 feet in height. Both to the north and south this plain of Boulder Clay is bounded by a low escarpment sloping gradually down to a low-land plain, more or less covered with peat, which form the other two areas into which the district may be naturally divided. That to the north, is bisected by the River Wyre, which has spread its alluvium over the low-lying tract lying between it, and the coast at Rossall That to the south though extremely small in the present sheet, is a portion of that great peat-covered lowland plain which has been described in the Memoirs and Explanations of 89 N.W., 90 N.E., and S.E., as sweeping round the entire coast of south-western Lancashire.

It is worthy of note, that both in the lowland plain of the Fylde, and that of S.W. Lancashire, the peat (though often 20 and even 30 feet in thickness, and occurring at depths of 50 and 60 feet below the present sea-level) is generally underlaid by a marine, post-glacial deposit, which in quarter-sheets 90 S.E, and 89 N.W., consists of the Shirdley Hill Sand, and in the present quarter-sheet of the Preesall Shingle; proving that before the growth of the peat, and the obstruction of drainage during which the land was higher than at present, considerable denudation of the Boulder Clay plain took place, cliffs were formed, at the foot of which these marine sands and shingles were deposited These cliffs, through the agency of sub-aerial agencies, have been gradually rounded so as to take the form now assumed by the lines of the Upper Boulder Clay escarpments, overlooking the peat-covered tracts, one of which forms the boundary between the Boulder Clay, and the Peat, near the Blackpool Station of the Lytham and Southshore Railway

The drainage of the peat plain, both in this and the map to the south (90 N.E), flows into the estuary of the Ribble, not by any particular brook, or water-course, but by a general soakage through the Sand Hills, and shingle fringing the beach. The peat plain also receives the drainage of the southern slopes, of the Glacial Drift hill, forming its northern margin, the watershed between the Ribble and Wyre running from Blackpool by Layton Hall, Great and Little Marton, to Great Plumpton. But between the last two hamlets, it crosses a col, or valley, which is continuously connected with one running to the Wyre at Skippool,* to the north, and with the Lytham peat-plain, extending to the Ribble. In fact the peat of the latter plain extends northward, being continuously connected with the peat found in the "col," as far as the parish boundary near Preese Hall.† From that point to Skippool, in the Wyre portion of the depression, the peat is concealed being covered over with silt and alluvium, in part brought down by floods, and in part brought up by the influence of the tides; the tract being known as Preese Hall Carrs, Todderstaff Hall Carrs, Singleton Carrs, Poulton and Little Poulton Carrs. The whole of the area is traversed by a sluice known as the Main Dyke, made some years ago to drain Marton Mere, which lake lies in another depression, or "clay basin" in the Glacial Drift, connected with the Preese Hall depression, by a "col" running from Mythorp Toll Gate, a distance of nearly a mile, to Preese Hall Carrs, with an average width of 130 yards, the level of the top of the dyke banks being only about 18 feet above the mean level of the sea. As this low level is continuously maintained to Skippool, and the alluvium is in many places more than 10 feet in thickness, it is clear that before the silt was deposited, tidal water could flow up the Skippool valley into that of Marton Mere; more especially during the period preceding the growth of the peat underlying the alluvium, which now occupies a depth of at least another ten feet.

Had the land stood in the period immediately preceding the growth of the peat at the same level as now, there must have been at least 12 feet of water in the Marton Mere depression; but as it is certain, from the occurrence of the "Preesall Hill shingle" below the peat, in the present map, and the presence of Shirdley Hill Sand, in a similar situation, in the district west of Ormskirk, that Western Lancashire stood at least 15 feet lower during that era than it does at present, it is clear that the depth of water in this valley, at high spring-tides, could not have been far short of 30 feet. This will account for the terraced appearance observable, on the adjacent bluffs, and for the fact that Boulder Clay at their bases, appears in several places to have been re-arranged, much of the clay having been removed and the stones left. This is particularly the case between Thatchplat Bridge, and the road from Little Marton, and Mythorp, where the stones are so plentiful, as to be dug for gravel.

These remarks would equally apply to the depression occupied by peat between Preese Hall Carrs, and Lytham Moss, for the level of the surface of the peat, along the line of lowest depression, nowhere exceeds 18 feet above the mean sea-level. It is therefore clear, that during the period of the deposition of the Preesall Hill shingle and Shirdley Hill sand there was a continuous connexion between the waters of the Ribble and the Wyre through the col, between Mythorp and Great Plumpton, and that at high tides the country around Poulton, Mythorp, Staining and Blackpool, was an island separated from the mainland by an isthmus, half a mile in width, and the Rossall and Lytham plains, which are now covered with peat and alluvium, being beneath the sea.

* Spelt "Shippool" on the one-inch Ordnance map.
† The area occupied by the peat in this col has been shown on the map, to a certain extent, by having the stippling for the hill-shading removed, at the bottom of the depression. In the edition of the map showing the surface geology, the boundaries of the various Drift Deposits are denoted by means of fine dotted lines.

By similar facts and reasoning a former connexion between the River Wyre at Rawcliffe and the estuary of the Lune at Pilling across the alluvial and peat plains east of Preesall and Stainall may be proved The drainage of this area is still much obstructed, it is carried by a sluice into Morecambe Bay near Pilling.

Geological Formations—The following strata are represented on the map:—

RECENT	-	{ Blown Sand. { Alluvium
TRIAS or NEW SANDSTONE	}	Keuper, or New Red Marls.

NEW RED SANDSTONE.

The only representative of this series so extensively developed in southern and south-western Lancashire are the Keuper Marls, the existence of which is proved by borings at Fleetwood and at Poulton in the Fylde, as well as the country to the south of the present map.

A boring at Poulton was made in search for coal, and after penetrating the Upper Boulder Clay, Middle Sand and Lower Boulder-Clay, passed through the red and grey marls (with much salt and gypsum) of the Keuper series without reaching their base for a depth of 179 yards

The boring at the North Euston Hotel, now the Barracks, at Fleetwood was made in search of water for the War authorities. It reached a depth of 189 yards, passing through sand and shingle, Boulder Clay, and Red Keuper Marls, when a bed of grit was struck, but not penetrated, no water was obtained.*

If the grit reached below the Keuper Marls was the Lower Keuper Sandstones, or "Waterstones," it is difficult to explain the absence of water, more especially as the sandstone maintains its water-bearing character in a district so near as the country around Waterloo, near Liverpool. In that district, however, the uppermost bed is often a hard compact grit with many round quartz pebbles without water, and it is possible that this bed was present at Fleetwood, and was not penetrated in the boring. At the same time it is possible that the whole of the Triassic and Permian beds below the Keuper Marls are absent in this area, and that the grit reached belonged to the Yoredale series This is borne out by the fact that in a well at Scarisbrick Park, east of Southport, the Red Marls were penetrated without coming to anything corresponding to Keuper Sandstone, the beds being stated to be shale, limestone, chert, and grit, apparently belonging to the Carboniferous Limestone Shales.

Two borings have been recently made in a field near Preesall After passing through the Boulder Clay, the Keuper Marls were reached, and in them a bed of rock salt was discovered, it is stated of a thickness of 30 feet, but on this head I was not able to obtain definite information when I visited the bore-hole.

DRIFT DEPOSITS.

The whole of the district within this map is covered with Glacial and Post-glacial Drifts, the older rocks being nowhere visible, in fact lying everywhere beneath the sea-level. Of these various Drifts, two only are represented on the map of the solid geology, the recent Alluvium and the Blown Sand; but the boundaries of all the Drift deposits were traced during the survey and are indicated by fine dotted lines on the map

* For details of this section, see Appendix to the "Description of Quarter Sheet 90 N E, and Explanation of the Country around Southport, Lytham, and Southshore."

The following are the subdivisions into which the Drifts were found to be capable of separation. the names being those used in the Explanation of maps 90 N E. and 90 S.E.

POST-GLACIAL.	Recent	Blown Sand. Upper " Cyclas " Clay, Sand, &c Upper " Scrobicularia " Clay Marsh Clay, and Tidal Alluvium	Alluvium
	Pre-historic	Peat. Lower " Cyclas " Clay. Lower " Scrobicularia " Clay Preesall Shingle.	Ancient Alluvium.
GLACIAL.	Glacial	Upper Boulder Clay Middle Sand and Shingle. Lower Boulder Clay	

GLACIAL DRIFTS.

Lower Boulder Clay.—From the termination of the peat plain of Lytham and South Shore to the commencement of the alluvial plain of Rossall and Fleetwood, run a range of cliffs, composed of Glacial Drift from 40 to 70 feet in height In their central and highest part they consist mainly of the sands and shingle beds of the Middle Drift, but to the north and to the south, at Norbreck and the Gynn respectively, the Upper Boulder Clay thickens, and its base gradually descends towards the sea-level, until, at length, at Cleveley's to the north and at South Shore to the south, its base is below low-water mark

At the base of these cliffs and on the beach below them, dome or arch-shaped masses of Lower Boulder Clay rise upwards into the Middle Sands at several points between the Gynn and Norbreck. The largest and most considerable of these is that at the base of the cliff, north and south of the termination of the lane leading to Bispham by Cradley Slack, extending about 270 yards to the north and 160 to the south, the clay disappearing under the Middle Sand and Gravel, at either end. A little south of the termination of the lane mentioned above, the clay rises about 25 feet in a low flat-topped arch, sinking in a hollow curve to about 8 feet below the lane, and rising again to 16 feet north of it. Between the clay and the sand above occurs a band of a greenish-coloured fine silt, attaining an average thickness of 8 inches which is tolerably persistent over the whole surface of the boss of Lower Boulder Clay, though here and there it is replaced by a bed of shingle cemented together by oxide of iron.

Towards the base of this deposit immediately above the beach, there appear to be two distinct beds, the lower exceedingly crowded with stones, most of them much rounded after having been previously scratched and separated from the upper bed by a sharp line of demarcation, apparently a line of stratification. In the centre of the section where the clay is thickest, the clay is entirely of one consistence without the slightest trace of bedding, with the exception of the upper surface, the flowing lines of which, covered with the band of fine green silty clay, is well seen in the section at Red Bank, near Norbreck. A section of this is given in the Memoir " On the Superficial Deposits of the country adjoining the coasts of south-west Lancashire " *

A great number of specimens of hæmatite iron ore have lately been found in the Lower Boulder Clay, exposed on the beach between tide-marks, opposite this section, which, coupled with the fact of the occurrence of similar fragments in the Upper Boulder Clay on the top of the

* Memoirs of the Geological Survey, 1875.

Cliff at Norbreck, has led to an erroneous idea of the possibility of iron ore being worked in the area to advantage.

Further south a mass of the Lower Boulder Clay rises some 5 or 6 feet above the beach near the gap in the cliff at Bank, where it is rather more sandy than the Cradley Slack boss and does not contain so many stones. It is of deep Indian-red colour, with often a yellowish tinge. Tracts of similar character occur in several parts of the beach between tide-marks, where they are bored into by pholades ; some of these patches occur between the two piers, and one south of that at South Shore. After the severe storm of March 1869 I found the whole of the beach at some distance from the land north of Blackpool, to consist of stiff clay with many erratic boulders and shells of *Turritella terebra*, &c., which I believe to belong to the lower division of the Drift.

Middle Sand.—This deposit is well seen in the railway-cuttings between Kirkham and Singleton, near Great Plumpton and Weeton In fact, commencing at the eastern edge of the map it occupies both sides of the railway cuttings as far as the Watch House at Weeton About 24 feet of sand is exposed, where thickest capped, by from 4 to 12 feet of Upper Boulder Clay, the base of the sand is wet, it is extremely pure, free from clay and of a bright-yellow colour, and contains very few stones. It is also seen in a sand pit between the railway and Great Plumpton, and between Great Plumpton and Westby Windmill in a brickfield, in the Upper Boulder Clay, where six feet of clay, resting on six feet of the sand which is current-bedded to the north-west, dipping two degrees. On the opposite side of the railway the Middle Sand crops to the surface at Whitprick Hill, (at the top of which is a reservoir of the Fylde Waterworks, 130 feet above the mean sea level,) at Weeton Windmill, and the Hall Hill west of the village. To the north the hamlet of Thistleton is built upon it, the sand extending 700 yards to the south and about 24 feet being visible. Also Little Eccleston Hall where 16 feet of sand is exposed.

The sand is well seen in the sand pits at Brackinscal and Singleton Windmill, near Great Singleton. It also crops out on the side of the hill at Great Holts, south of Poulton-in-the-Fylde ; the Upper Boulder Clay caps the top of the hill, and also covers the lower slope below the out-crop of the Middle Sand.

To the west the village of Great Marton is built upon the sand, which is well seen in the pits on the south side of the road, capped by a few feet of stiff compact chocolate-coloured Upper Boulder Clay, which is there about 22 feet thick, but the base, of course, is not seen ; it is current-bedded to the S.S.E. and contains a good many pebbles lying in the planes of oblique lamination.

North of Layton a tract of Middle Sand crops to the surface for a distance of several yards along the road side, not less than 30 feet being visible, somewhat interbedded with thin seams of silty clay a few inches thick.

At the nunnery near Little Layton, a well was sunk, which at the time of my visit was in the sands and shingles below the Upper Boulder Clay. Northward of this the Upper Clay forms the whole surface of the country on the west side of the River Wyre, except where it is covered with Post-glacial Deposits ; but on the east bank of the Wyre below Knot End, is a cliff called Hackinsall Brows, between sea-mark and land-mark, near the latter between tide-mark, the Boulder Clay visible upon the beach, probably belongs to the lower division.

The Middle Sand is also visible at the top of the small hill immediately east of New Heys Farm, and it also crops at the top of Preesall Hill in this area. The sands beneath the clay have evidently an undulating surface, rising from 16 feet above high-water mark at Hackinsall Brow to the top of Preesall Hill.

Very fine sections of the Middle Sands are exposed in the cliff-section between Gynn and Norbreck ; the beds being not less than 60 feet in thickness, and the sands being current-bedded to the S S.E Many shells occur both in the sands and in the shingle-beds, lists of which are given in the Survey Memoirs on the Superficial Geology of the country adjoining the coasts of south-west Lancashire.

There are, I am informed by Mr. Gorst, several tolerably deep wells in Blackpool, one of which is in the market, but the particulars of the beds through which they were made have not been preserved. The water seam is a little above spring-tide high-water mark, and probably occurs at the base of the Upper Boulder Clay which dips westerly as well as southerly.

Upper Boulder Clay.—This deposit, though seldom seen in section from the level nature of the country and the close character of the grass that grows upon it, occupies the largest area of any surface-deposit in Western Lancashire.

From the extremely impermeable nature of the clay, the rain-fall drains off it towards lower levels, little sinking into the ground ; while springs are extremely rare, and occur only on the outcrop of bands of sand.

To supply the cattle and sheep with water, ponds, locally called pits, are dug in the ground, in which the rain collects. Much of the material excavated consists of marl, which from the decomposition of Mountain Limestone, boulders, and other causes, is often sufficiently calcareous to be used in marling the adjacent peat-lands When the bed is good these " marl pits " often reach a considerable size and are excavated down to the Middle Sand and Shingle beneath, which owing to the percolation, of lime-charged water, is often cemented together, so as to form a material, at first sight closely resembling the Kinderscout Millstone Grit. Some characteristic blocks of this consolidated shingle occur at the base of Norbreck Cliffs, and two very large masses form the Penny and Carling stones, exposed at low spring tides off Norbreck and Bispham.

East of Blackpool the Upper Boulder Clay has an average thickness of 30 or 40 feet. The upper beds, seen east of Preston, appear here to have been denuded away Along the coast line, in the cliffs of Norbreck, the clay is even thinner, ranging from 7 to 20 feet. It sometimes is traversed by vertical planes or joints separating it into slightly columnar masses, and exhibits slight traces of bedding in a S.S.E. direction. Fragments and occasionally perfect specimens of several shells of Mollusca occur, including the species *Turritella terebra,* *Cardium edule,* and *Tellina Balthica.*

A few seams of sand, resembling that of the Middle Sand, are in a few places intercalated, but I failed to find any shells in these beds.

South of Blackpool, the Upper Boulder Clay is well seen, at several points, on the road to Walker's Hill. At the latter place, three feet of dark-red clay rests on a band of blue marl, four inches thick, lying on six feet of light-red clay ; and at Hay's Side Common 12 feet of very dark clay is exposed, the dark colour of which may be due to the clay hills along this line of country being supersaturated with water.

The following towns, villages, hamlets, and farms are on the Upper Boulder Clay ·—Blackpool, Poulton-le-Fylde, Layton, Staining, Newton, Little Marton, Mythorp, Dagger's Hole, Great Plumpton, Weeton, Swarbrick Hall, Hardhorn, Warbreck, Forshaws Hill, Great and Little Carleton, Bispham, Norbreck, Thornton, Great and Little Singleton, Hambleton, Stainall, Crombleholmes, Stalmine, and Preesall.

The number of " clay basins," or saucer-shaped depressions, in the

Upper Boulder Clay, in the area between Blackpool, Poulton, and Staining, is the marked feature of this country. Nearly all of them, from rising towards what should be the outlet, enclose a certain portion of the drainage which runs into them; the excess waters only running away when the water has risen above the level of the outlet. This obstruction to the drainage has caused nearly all these swamp-hollows to be filled in with peat, occasionally lying on lacustrine marls. In this district, as well as in the country north of Preston, these hollows are entirely formed in the glacial deposits, and the rock surface is invariably at a considerable depth from the bottom of the hollow, trending, like the surface of the drift, in an inclined plane from the east towards the west, or from the Grit Fells of Chipping, in the next map (91 S.W.), to the sea at Blackpool. The Drift-deposits which thin out at Chipping, at an elevation of about 500 feet, at Blackpool are still nearly 100 feet above the average sea-level; while the rock-plain, starting from the same elevation at Chipping, is at the very least 20 feet below the sea-level at the sea-coast. The fall of the rock-plain is therefore more steep than that of the Drift by at least 120 feet, the whole of the intervening space being filled up with Drift of that thickness.

It is therefore probable that the extensive Drift-plain of Western Lancashire, a portion of which is comprised within the present map, owes its origin to the deposition of Glacial Deposits during subsidence upon an old rock-plain of marine denudation, the eastern limit of which formed a bay running from near Rufford, by Eccleston, Euxton, Bamber Bridge, Samelsbury, the Ribble valley, Broughton, Garstang, and Cockerham, to Morecambe Bay; westward of which line the rock surface is either but little above, at, and often below the sea-level, though the surface of this tract of country often rises to a height of 170 feet from the superposition of Glacial Drift. If it be admitted that the surface of the latter owes its inclination to deposition and not to denudation, it is easy to understand that the surface, within certain limits, would be subject to undulation, and that hollows would be left, the level of the entrances to which would be often above that of the central portion of the depression. This would explain the fact that when these clay-basins are numerous, as at Carleton, they are invariably connected with each other by dry cols, having no connexion with the lines of drainage of the country.

The level of the base of the Upper Boulder Clay, at its junction with the Middle Drift, rises from 40 feet above the mean level of the sea, at the Gynn, to seventy feet at a point a few yards south of the lane to Bispham, sinking again to 20, and eventually entirely disappearing beneath the sea-level at Norbreck, north of which the Upper Boulder Clay forms the substratum of the various Post-glacial Deposits between that hamlet and Fleetwood. It is clear, therefore, that the surface of the Middle Drift, like that of the Lower Boulder Clay beneath it, in the section exposed in the cliffs between Blackpool, has an arched or domed-shaped form, dipping north and south respectively; the latter trend carrying the base of the Upper Boulder Clay well under the town of Blackpool, causing the whole of that town to be situated on the clay. The sand, however, nearly reaches the surface in the fields beyond the Queen's Hotel, being at the bottom of several ponds (locally called "pits") dug in the clay. In a boring near one of these fields, the Blackpool Cemetery, now being laid out, two thin beds of Boulder Clay, with an intercalated bed of sand, overlaid the Middle Drift.[*]

---

* For the journal of this boring, I have to thank Mr Gorst, the surveyor to the Local Board.

The Upper Sand (bed 2), I observed cropping to the surface for a distance of six yards, a little east of the cemetery, and again for five yards a little west of the culvert, at the junction of the Marton road with the Poulton and Blackpool roads : it then graduates into gravel, and contains fragments of shells of the species *Turritella terebra, Cardium edule,* and *Tellina Balthica.*

OLDER POST-GLACIAL DEPOSITS.

Preesall Hill Shingle.—This deposit is well seen in several shallow pits lying at the foot of the steep cliff or bluff called Preesall Hill, especially in one a few yards west of the cottage Little Tongues. Here I found fragments of hæmatite iron-ore and of Permian Red Sandstone, probably derived from the opposite side of Morecambe Bay; and the shells of several species of Mollusca, including *Cardium edule, C. rusticum, Purpura lapillus, Natica monilifera,* and *Turritella terebra*, the rounded character of the pebbles and the species of the shells indicating the beach-margin of a shallow sea.

Peat and grey *Scrobicularia* Clay overlap and cover these old gravels over a large area, extending far into the next map, 91 S.E., and occupying a similar position to the Shirdley Hill Sand, which underlies the peat of similar age in the district lying between the rivers Mersey and Ribble, described in the "Explanations of Maps 90 S.E. and N.E.," indicating a period when the great lowland plains, since covered with peat, were at least 20 feet lower than at present.

Lower Scrobicularia Clay is seen in several ditches and sluices beneath the peat, at the foot of Preesall Hill, near the Shingle beds described above ; it probably extends eastward, but the base of the peat is not seen

Lower Cyclas Clay.—South of Blackpool the Boulder Clay tract at South Shore gives place to the peat-covered plain, only a very small portion of which is shown on the map. After the severe storm of March 1869, I examined the coast, and found the Southshore embankment, then in course of construction, to be wasted away, and a thick bed of peat exposed, capped by blown sand, and resting on a bed of grey clay, full of rushes and the stems of other marsh plants. From the fresh-water character of the clay, and its position beneath the thick peat, it would appear to be on the same horizon as the Lower Cyclas Clay south of the Ribble

Peat.—The largest area occupied by peat in this map is Preesall Moss extending from Preesall Park eastwards to the margin of the map, and southwards from the alluvium at Pointer House and New England to Hankinson House. Southwards of that point it is much broken up by islets of Boulder Clay, which are surrounded by peat, which gradually narrow to an eighth of a mile at Whip Lane End, where it passes below the alluvium to the Wyre.

Another layer of peat occupies the bottom of the long swamp-valley, which extending from the Wyre at Skippool, to near Lytham in the estuary of the Ribble, forms a col in the watershed dividing those two rivers.

Several other patches of peat occupy swamp-hollows as that of Whitemoss Gap, which is connected by hollows or furrows, with the alluvium of Marton Mere which rests on peat -

Alluvium.—The considerable tract coloured as alluvium on the northern portion of the map consists of tidal silt, and salt marsh-clay, graduating into ordinary brook-alluvium, occurring at the bottom of the shallow valleys in the Boulder Clay, around Bispham, between Cleveley's and Poulton Breck, and at several spots, on the eastern side of the Wyre ;

notably between Fern Hill House and Park Cottage, near Preesall Park, and west of the knoll of Boulder Clay, on which the village of Preesall is built. East of this village, the alluvium does not abut against the low hills of Boulder Clay, as it does on the west side; but it gradually thins out to the south and rests on the peat, which underlies the alluvial clay to the north even where it is thickest.

The Blown Sand of Fleetwood rests upon this tidal alluvium, but to the west the sand hills are underlaid by shingle mixed with silty clay, and sand, which is well seen as the cemetery. Still further west, however, near Rossall, the blown sand, which has nearly thinned out, rests upon beds of yellowish clay, which were manufactured some years ago, into bricks, used in the adjacent embankments, and sea walls, since unfortunately almost entirely destroyed. In the course of digging the excavations for the clay, a great number of Roman coins were found at a depth* of eight feet from the surface, which latter is about 22 feet above the Ordnance datum, the level of the coins being therefore about two feet above high-water mark.

Further to the south near Flakefleet House, the alluvium consists of stiff yellow clay, becoming dark and dense at a depth of 20 to 22 feet, resting on shingle. In the dark clay, occur a great number of shells of the species *Scrobicularia piperata, Cardium edule,* and *Tellina Balthica.* I am inclined to think that the shingle occurring below this alluvium, is of the age of the Preesall shingle underlying the peat, and that the latter deposit has been for the most denuded away by the scour of the Wyre when it flowed westward to the sea by Rossall, before the deposition of the tidal mud and later shingle. This view is borne out, to a certain extent, by the boring for an artesian well made at Fleetwood, which passed through sand, shingle, and boulder clay, but no peat. The Boulder Clay now spreads as a sheet under the whole of the neck of land from Bispham to Fleetwood, and under the Wyre water, for it not only comes up from beneath tidal alluvium at the small island east of Hame Lake, but it is seen at low tide, in a gap in the old railway, and present embankment, just east of the letter 't' in "Wyre Water" in the one-inch map, where it is covered by nearly 30 feet of silty clays. The Boulder Clay is also seen underlying the peat and grey clay, on the sea-shore between Cleveley's and Rossall land-mark, and the former rises in many abrupt knolls, or hillocks, from the alluvial plain, as at Willcocks, Thornton, Holmes, Poolfoot, Bourne Hall, and Steyna.

To the south it was reached in a well, made near the Wesleyan Chapel, in Ramper Road, (leading from Cleveley's Station to Cleveleys) at a depth of seven and a half yards, at which depth a tolerably plentiful supply of brackish water was afforded. The level of the surface of the ground here is about 14 feet (that of the Boulder Clay would therefore be six and a half feet) below the Ordnance datum-line, or about six feet above that of low-water springs, and the surface of the country only from two to three feet above high-water mark. Westward between Haddle House and Whitecar House, the alluvial sandy clay, is underlaid by a peaty clay, resting on a light-blue clay. A little further south, the two latter deposits thin out, the ordinary alluvium rests on a reddish-yellow Upper Boulder Clay; the alluvium becoming almost pure sand at Bridge End House, which narrows to a mere neck 25 yards broad at Churchtown, but again spreads at Bispham. It there consists of a coarse red gravel, mixed with sand,

---

* For the information as to the depth at which the coins occurred, I have to thank Mr. Bond, of Fleetwood railway-station. The position in which the coins were found was recorded by the Ordnance Survey, on their six-inch map.

about eight feet thick, for the occurrence of which it is not easy to account, the present small brook being quite incapable of moving many of the included stones, though it may have been able to do so, when its fall was greater, it having now reached its lowest possible plane of denudation.

Blown Sand.—The largest tract of Blown Sand in the map, under consideration is that between Fleetwood, and Rossall land-mark, where sand dunes rise to a height of 20 to 30 feet.

The sand is extremely large-grained, derived from pebbles on the beach, which are mainly made up from the detritus of igneous rocks brought from the Boulder Clay cliffs by tidal currents from the south. The highest point amongst the sand hills, is that called "The Mount," a little west of Fleetwood, which rises to a height of about 70 feet, which hillock however is fast being worn away by the action of the sea, the terrace walk on the seaward side of the Mount, existing at the time of the Ordnance Survey being made having entirely disappeared. In fact since that period (1846), not less than 50 yards has been worn away, giving an average of 2½ yards per year, and that in the very highest ground, Norbreck cliffs and Morecambe Bay.

A low tract of Blown Sand, never however rising into dunes, skirts the shore of the bay, from Knot end to Pilling. At Parrox Hall Park an ancient mound sixteen feet high composed of made ground with a small quantity of charcoal occurs on this sand.

From Rossall land-mark southwards towards Fenny,* the Blown Sand thins out, and the alluvial clay extends to the coast; it is capped however from opposite Larkholm to Rossall by a narrow bank of shingle or storm-beach, which, at the latter place, is covered with blown sand, extending southward as far as Carr House (deserted at the time of the survey, August 1869) From this point to Willcocks, the Blown Sand rests on Upper Boulder Clay, which at the latter place rises to the surface and forms a knoll.

From Cleveleys to Angersholme, the belt of Blown Sand increases in width, covering the seaward edges of the flat alluvial fields, which alluvium finds its southern termination against the rising slope of the Upper Boulder Clay, which extends continuously from Angersholme and Bispham House by Norbreck and Blackpool to the peat-plain of Lytham and Southshore. The slope of the surface of the Boulder Clay gradually rises southward, until its greatest cliff-elevation is reached at Bank (105 feet), and the adjacent inlier at Knowles and Warbreck (118 feet). The top of the sea-cliff is more or less covered with Blown Sand from Angersholme to Norbreck Lodge, extending inland for a distance of 250 yards opposite Bispham Lodge. The following is the section exposed in the cliff, where the lane from Bispham House, reaches the beach :—

```
1 Blown Sand              - 3 feet 0 in
2. Cemented shingle and iron  - 2  ,,  0 ,,
3. Gravelly Sand          0  ,,  3 ,,
4. Yellow Sand            1  ,,  8 ,,
5 Red Loam               1  ,,  0 ,,
6 Upper Boulder Clay     1  ,,  0 ,,
```

Two hundred yards further north, the section is as follows :—

```
1. Blown Sand            - 10 feet 0 in.
1a Loam                  - 0  ,,  6 ,,
1b. Peaty bed            - 0  ,,  9 ,,
1c Loam                  - 1  ,,  0 ,,
2. Gravel                - 2  ,,  0 ,,
```

* Or rather towards its site, the house is entirely washed away

Fifty yards south of the first section, the following beds are seen :—

1 Sand	-	- 4 feet	1 Sand	-	2 feet
2. Ferruginous Gravel		2 „	6. Upper Boulder Clay -		8 „
5. Loam	-	- 3 „	(Scratched Stones.)		
6 Clay	-	- 4 „			

From these sections the undulating character of the surface of the Boulder Clay may be noted, the occurrence of peaty and loamy beds of fresh-water origin in these hollows, and that of ferruginous gravel or shingle below them, probably of the age of the Preesall Shingle, and thrown down by the sea before the growth of peat on the lowlands.

The face of the lower slope of the cliff, north of the lane from Cradley Slack, is much concealed by blown sand, causing a slight local gain of land, the surface of the sand having become overgrown with the sand reed or "starr-grass."

At the top of the high cliff, between Bank and Uncle Tom's Cabin, a deposit of fine sand occurs, from four to nine feet in thickness, blown from the "Middle Sand" forming the face of the cliff, during high winds. A much greater thickness of sand would be accumulated were it not continually dug and carted away.

APPENDIX.

The following is a list of some of the larger boulders in the Upper Boulder Clay, occurring within the area comprised in the map, or in the country immediately adjoining, and of the parentage of stones of smaller size :—

The sheets are those of the six-inch Map of Lancashire

Sheet 59 At Robbins, Porphyry, 6 × 3½ × 3 feet
At the Fold, Trap, 4 × 3 × 3 feet.

At Little Marton Windmill, at the brickfield, the Upper Boulder Clay contained—

Granite	-	-	1
Permian Breccia	-		4
Quartz rock	-		4
Lake district "volcanic series"			32
Silurian grits	-		52
			100

Sheet 51 Old Bank Field—

Old Red Sandstone			1
Trap	-		3
Carboniferous Limestone	-		12
Lake District volcanic series			28
Granite	-	-	20
Silurian grits	-	-	36
			100

In the Boulder Clay Cliff of the River Wyre adjacent—

Carboniferous Limestone	-		5
Silurian grits	-		15
Granite	-		2
Volcanic series	-	-	3
			25

Little Singleton —Angular boulder of volcanic breccia
4 × 4 × 3 feet = 48 cubic feet, weighing about 4 tons

An examination of the Pebbles on Blackpool beach gave :—

Carboniferous grit	- 4
Limestones, 1 black, 1 red, rest grey	- 12
Felspathic ash	- 4
Hornstone	- 1
Silurian grits	- 5
Amygdaloidal ash	- 1
Trap and altered breccia	- 54
Granites	- 20
	100

BLACKPOOL CLIFFS. (Upper Boulder Clay.) (Determined by Mr. Binney. Mem. Lit. Phil. Soc. vol. x p. 132)

Granite, Greenstones	49 per cent.
Slates and Silurians	32 ,,
Mountain Limestone	6 ,,
Coal measures	9 ,,
New Red Sandstone, lias, and chalk	4 ,,
Striated rocks, chiefly Silurian slates and grits	6 ,,

} 15 per cent.

List of the highest altitudes occurring in this Quarter Sheet.

Beryl Ihll, Trigonometrical Station	117 feet
Blackpool Cemetery	45 ,,
Layton, north side	75 ,,
Great Marton	55 ,,
Singleton Church	79 ,,
Singleton Windmill	58 ,,
Brackinscal	70 ,,
Poulton Holts	70 ,,
Weeton Windmill	132 ,,
Weeton Hall Hill	103 ,,
Great Plumpton Railway	80 ,,
Whitprick Hill	125 ,,
Thiselton	70 ,,
Little Eccleston Hall	55 ,,
Thornton Trigonometrical Station	49 ,,
Poulton Windmill	40 ,,
Poulton Market Cross	48 ,,
Preesall Hill, Trigonometrical Station	106 ,,

List of some of the lowest altitudes occurring in this Quarter Sheet, given in the Ordnance Survey Abstracts of Levelling   London, 1861

Bench Mark on east pier of Skippool Bridge, at junction of roads, 2 54 feet below top of parapet	18·92 feet
Bolt in north side of Thornton Windmill ; 3 00 feet above surface	18 91 ,,
Mark on south pier of gate to Flakefleet House farm yard , 3·87 feet above surface	20 81 ,,
Mark on wall in front of Lower Shore Light House ; 4 72 feet above surface	22 73 ,,
Zero of Tidge gauge, opposite Lower Shore Light House, Fleetwood (below Ordnance datum)	12·80

LONDON:

Printed by GEORGE E EYRE and WILLIAM SPOTTISWOODE,
Printers to the Queen's most Excellent Majesty
For Her Majesty's Stationery Office.

[4209 —250 —7/75]

LIST OF GEOLOGICAL MAPS, SECTIONS, AND PUBLICATIONS OF THE GEOLOGICAL SURVEY OF THE UNITED KINGDOM.

THE Maps are those of the Ordnance Survey, geologically coloured by the Geological Survey of Great Britain and Ireland under the Superintendence of Prof. A. C. RAMSAY, LL.D , F R S , &c , Director-General The various Formations are traced and coloured in all their Subdivisions.

ENGLAND AND WALES.—(Scale one-inch to a mile.)

Maps, Nos 3 to 41, 44, 64, price 8s. 6d. each, with the exceptions of 2, 10, 23, 24, 27, 28, 29, 32, 33, 39, 58, 4s. each. Sheets divided into four quarters, (1 N.W , N.E , S.W., S E), 42, 43, 45, 46, 52, 53, 54, 55, 56, 57, (59 N E., S.E.), 60, 61, 62, 63, 71, 72, 73, 74, 75, (76 N S), (77 N), 78, 79, 80, 81, 82, 88, 89, 105 (87 N.E , S.E.), 88 (90 S.E , N.E.), (91 S.W , 93 S W , N.W.), (98 N E , S E), (109 S E) Price 3s Except (57 N.W.), 76 (N.), (77 N.E.) Price 1s 6d.

SCOTLAND.—Maps 3, 7, 14, 22, 24, 32, 33, 34, 40, 41, 6s each Maps 1, 13, 4s.

IRELAND.—Maps 21, 23, 36, 37, 48, 49, 56, 61, 72, 74, 75, 78 to 92, and from 95 to 205, price 3s. each, with the exception of 38, 50 72, 82, 122, 131, 140, 156, 159, 160, 176, 180, 181, 182, 180, 190, 196, 197, 202, 203, 204, 205, price 1s 6d each

HORIZONTAL SECTIONS, Illustrative of the Geological Maps.

1 to 97, England, price 5s. each 1 to 57, Scotland, price 5s each. 1 to 23, Ireland, price 5s. each.

VERTICAL SECTIONS, Illustrative of Horizontal Sections and Maps

1 to 58, England, price 3s. 6d. each. 1, Ireland, price 3s. 6d. 1 to 3, Scotland, price 3s. 6d.

Memoirs of the Geological Survey and of the Museum of Practical Geology.

REPORT on CORNWALL, DEVON, and WEST SOMERSET By Sir H. T. DE LA BECHE, F R S , &c. 8vo 14s.
FIGURES and DESCRIPTIONS of the PALÆOZOIC FOSSILS in the above Counties. By PROFESSOR PHILLIPS, F.R.S. 8vo (Out of print.)
THE MEMOIRS of the GEOLOGICAL SURVEY of GREAT BRITAIN, and of the MUSEUM of ECONOMIC GEOLOGY of LONDON. 8vo. Vol. I. 21s. ; Vol. II. (in 2 Parts), 42s
The GEOLOGY of NORTH WALES. By PROFESSOR RAMSAY, LL.D. With an Appendix, by J. W. SALTER, A.L.S. Price 13s boards (Vol III , Memoirs, &c) (Out of print.)
The GEOLOGY of the LONDON BASIN. Part I. The Chalk and the Eocene Beds of the Southern and Western Tracts. By W WHITAKER, B A (Parts by H. W BRISTOW, F.R.S., and T MC K. HUGHES, M.A.) Price 13s boards. Vol IV.
BRITISH ORGANIC REMAINS. Decades I. to XIII., with 10 Plates each. MONOGRAPH No 1. On the Genus Pterygotus. By PROFESSOR HUXLEY, F.R.S., and J W. SALTER, F.G S Royal 4to. 4s. 6d. or royal 8vo. 2s. 8d. each Decade.
MONOGRAPH No 2 On the Structure of Belemnitidæ By PROFESSOR HUXLEY, LL.D., &c 2s 6d
RECORDS of the SCHOOL OF MINES and of SCIENCE applied to the ARTS Vol. I., in four Parts.
CATALOGUE of SPECIMENS in the Museum of Practical Geology, illustrative of the Composition and Manufacture of British Pottery and Porcelain By Sir HENRY DE LA BECHE, and TRENHAM REEKS, Curator. 8vo. 155 Woodcuts. 2nd Edition, by TRENHAM REEKS and F W RUDLER. Price 1s. 6d in wrapper, 2s in boards
A DESCRIPTIVE GUIDE to the MUSEUM of PRACTICAL GEOLOGY, with Notices of the Geological Survey of the United Kingdom, the School of Mines, and the Mining Record Office. By ROBERT HUNT, F.R.S., and F. W RUDLER. Price 6d. (3rd Edition.)
A DESCRIPTIVE CATALOGUE of the ROCK SPECIMENS in the MUSEUM of PRACTICAL GEOLOGY. By A C. RAMSAY, F.R.S., H. W. BRISTOW, F.R.S., H BAUERMAN, and A. GEIKIE, F.G.S. Price 1s. (3rd Edit.)
On the TERTIARY FLUVIO-MARINE FORMATION of the ISLE of WIGHT. By EDWARD FORBES, F.R.S. Illustrated with a Map and Plates of Fossils, Sections, &c. Price 5s.
On the GEOLOGY of the COUNTRY around CHELTENHAM Illustrating Sheet 44. By E. HULL, A.B Price 2s 6d.
On the GEOLOGY of PARTS of WILTSHIRE and GLOUCESTERSHIRE (Sheet 34) By A C. RAMSAY, F.G S , W. T. AVELINE, F G S , and EDWARD HULL, B.A., F.G S. Price 3d.
On the GEOLOGY of the SOUTH STAFFORDSHIRE COAL-FIELD. By J. B. JUKES, M.A., F.R.S. (3rd Edit.) 3s. 6d.
On the GEOLOGY of the WARWICKSHIRE COAL-FIELD. By H.H HOWELL, F G S 1s 6d.
On the GEOLOGY of the COUNTRY around WOODSTOCK. Illustrating Sheet 45 S.W. By E. HULL, A.B. 1s.
On the GEOLOGY of the COUNTRY around PRESCOT, LANCASHIRE. By EDWARD HULL, A.B., F.G.S. (2nd Edition.) Illustrating Quarter Sheet, No 80 N W. Price 3d.
On the GEOLOGY of PART of LEICESTERSHIRE By W. TALBOT AVELINE, F G S , and H. H. HOWELL, F.G.S. Illustrating Quarter Sheet, No. 63 S.E Price 3d.
On the GEOLOGY of PART of NORTHAMPTONSHIRE. Illustrating Sheet 53 S.E. By W. T. AVELINE, F G.S., and RICHARD TRENCH, B.A., F G S Price 3d
On the GEOLOGY of the ASHBY-DE-LA-ZOUCH COAL-FIELD By EDWARD HULL, A.B., F G S Illustrating Sheets 63 N.W and 71 S W. Price 3s.
On the GEOLOGY of PARTS of OXFORDSHIRE and BERKSHIRE. By E. HULL, A.B., and W. WHITAKER, B.A. Illustrating Sheet 13. Price 3s. (Out of print)
On the GEOLOGY of PARTS of NORTHAMPTONSHIRE and WARWICKSHIRE. By W T. AVELINE, F.G.S. Illustrating Quarter Sheet 53 N.E. 3d.
On the GEOLOGY of the COUNTRY around WIGAN. By EDWARD HULL, A.B., F.G.S. Illustrating Sheet 89 S.W. on the One-inch Scale, and Sheets 84, 85, 92, 93, 100, 101 on the Six-inch Scale, Lancashire. (2nd Edition) Price 1s
On the GEOLOGY of TRINIDAD (West Indian Surveys). By G P. WALL and J.G. SAWKINS, F.G.S., with Maps and Sections 12s.
On the GEOLOGY of JAMAICA (West Indian Surveys). By J.G SAWKINS, &c With Maps & Sections 8vo 1871. Price 9s.
COUNTRY around ALTRINCHAM, CHESHIRE. By E. HULL, B A Illustrating 80 N.E. Price 8d.
GEOLOGY of PARTS of NOTTINGHAMSHIRE and DERBYSHIRE. By W T. AVELINE, F G S. Illustrating 82 S.E. Price 8d.
COUNTRY around NOTTINGHAM By W. T AVELINE, F G S. Illustrating 71 N E Price 8d.
The GEOLOGY of PARTS of NOTTINGHAMSHIRE, YORKSHIRE, and DERBYSHIRE. Illustrating Sheet 82 N.E. By W. TALBOT AVELINE, F.G.S. Price 8d.
The GEOLOGY of SOUTH BERKSHIRE and NORTH HAMPSHIRE. Illustrating Sheet 12 By H. W. BRISTOW and W WHITAKER. Price 3s.
The GEOLOGY of the ISLE of WIGHT, from the WEALDEN FORMATION to the HEMPSTEAD BEDS inclusive, with Illustrations, and a List of the Fossils. Illustrating Sheet 10 By H.W. BRISTOW, F.R.S Price 6s.
The GEOLOGY of EDINBURGH. Illustrating Sheet 32 (Scotland). Price 4s By H. H. HOWELL and A GEIKIE
The GEOLOGY of the COUNTRY around BOLTON, LANCASHIRE By E HULL, B.A. Illustrating Sheet 89 S.E. Price 2s.
The GEOLOGY of BERWICK. Illustrating Sheet 34 Scotland. 1 inch By A. GEIKIE. Price 2s.
The GEOLOGY of the COUNTRY around OLDHAM By E HULL, B.A Illustrating 88 S W. Price 2s.
The GEOLOGY of PARTS of MIDDLESEX, &c Illustrating Sheet 7. By W. WHITAKER, B.A. Price 2s.
The GEOLOGY of the COUNTRY around BANBURY, WOODSTOCK, and BUCKINGHAM. Sheet 45. By A. H. GREEN, M.A. Price 2s.
The GEOLOGY of the COUNTRY between FOLKESTONE and RYE. By J. DREW, F G S (Sheet 4) Price 1s
The GEOLOGY of EAST LOTHIAN, &c (Maps 30, 34, 41, Scot) By H. H. HOWELL, F.G.S., A. GEIKIE, F R S , and J. YOUNG, M.D With an Appendix on the Fossils by J. W. SALTER, A.L.S.
The GEOLOGY of part of the YORKSHIRE COAL-FIELD (88 S E.) By A. H. GREEN, M.A. J. R. DAKYNS, M.A., and J. C. WARD, F.G.S. Oct 1869. 1s.
The GEOLOGY of the COUNTRY between LIVERPOOL and SOUTHPORT (90 S.E) By C. E. DE RANCE, F.G.S. Oct 1868. 3d.
The GEOLOGY of the COUNTRY around SOUTHPORT, LYTHAM, and SOUTH SHORE By C. E DE RANCE, F.G.S.
The GEOLOGY of the CARBONIFEROUS ROCKS NORTH and EAST of LEEDS, and the PERMIAN and TRIASSIC ROCKS about TADCASTER. By W. T. AVELINE, F.G.S., A. H GREEN, M.A., J R. DAKYNS, M.A., J C. WARD, F.G.S., and R RUSSELL. 8d
The GEOLOGY of the NEIGHBOURHOOD of KIRKBY LONSDALE and KENDAL. By W. T. AVELINE, F.G.S.,

THE COAL-FIELDS OF THE UNITED KINGDOM ARE ILLUSTRATED BY THE FOLLOWING PUBLISHED MAPS OF THE GEOLOGICAL SURVEY.

COAL-FIELDS OF UNITED KINGDOM.
(Illustrated by the following Maps.)

Anglesey, 78 (SW)
Bristol and Somerset, 19, 35
Coalbrook Dale, 61 (NE & SE)
Clee Hill, 53 (NE, NW).
Denbighshire, 74 (NE & SE), 79 (SE).
Derby and Yorkshire, 71 (NW, NE, & SE), 82 (NW & SW), 81 (NE), 87 (NE, SE), 88 (SE).
Flintshire, 79 (NE & SE).
Forest of Dean, 43 (SE & SW)
Forest of Wyre, 61 (SE), 55 (NE).
*Lancashire, 80 (NW), 81 (NW), 89 (SE, NE, NW, & SW), 88 (SW). (For corresponding six-inch Maps, see detailed list.)
*Leicestershire, 71 (SW), 63 (NW)
Newcastle, 105 (NE & SE)
*North Staffordshire, 72 (NW), 72 (SW), 73 (NE), 80 (SE), 81 (SW)
*South Staffordshire, 54 (NW), 62 (SW)
Shrewsbury, 60 (NE), 61 (NW & SW).
*South Wales, 86, 37, 38, 40, 41, 42 (SE, SW).
*Warwickshire, 62 (NE & SE), 63 (NW & SW), 54 (NE), 53 (NW)
Yorkshire, 88, 87 (SW), 93 (SW).

SCOTLAND.
*Edinburgh, 32, 33.   *Haddington, 32, 33
Fife and Kinross, 40, 41.

IRELAND.
*Kanturk, 174, 175   *Castlecomer, 128, 137.
*Killenaule (Tipperary), 146
(For Sections illustrating these Maps, see detailed list.)
* With descriptive Memoir.

GEOLOGICAL MAPS OF ENGLAND AND SCOTLAND.
Scale, six inches to a mile
The Coalfields of Lancashire, Northumberland, Durham, Yorkshire, Edinburghshire, Haddingtonshire, Fifeshire, and Ayrshire are being surveyed on a scale of six inches to a mile   Price 6s

Lancashire.
47. Clitheroe
48. Colne, Twiston Moor
49. Laneshaw Bridge   Horiz. Sect. 62, partly illustrates this sheet
55. Whalley
56. Haggate. 6s   Horiz. Sect 62, 65
57. Winewall.
62. Balderstone, &c.
63. Accrington.
64. Burnley
65. Stiperden Moor   4s.
70. Blackburn, &c
71. Haslingden
72. Cliviger, Bacup, &c.
73. Todmorden   4s
78. Bolton-le-Moors
79. Entwistle
80. Tottington.
81. Wardle   6s   —   Horiz. Sect. 66   Illustrates the sheet.
84. Ormskirk, St John's, &c.
85. Standish, &c
86. Adlington, Herwick, &c. -   ,,   68   ,,
87. Bolton-le-Moors   -   ,,   67.   ,,
88. Bury Heywood   -   ,,   66   ,,
89. Rochdale, &c   -   ,,   66.   ,,
92. Bickerstaffe, Skelmersdale.
93. Wigan, Up Holland, &c   ,,   68.   ,,
94. West Houghton, Hindley, Atherton   -   ,,   67   ,,
95. Radcliffe, Peel Swinton, &c.   ,,   66–67.   ,,
96. Middleton, Prestwich, &c   ,,   66.   ,,
97. Oldham, &c   -   ,,   64   ,,
100. Knowsley, Rainford, &c.   -   ,,   67–68.   ,,
101. Billinge, Ashton, &c.   -   ,,   68   ,,
102. Leigh, Lowton   -   ,,   67   ,,
103. Ashley, Eccles   -   ,,   66   ,,
104. Manchester, Salford, &c. -   ,,   64–65   ,,
105. Ashton-under-Lyne   -   ,,   64–65   ,,
106. Liverpool, &c.   -   ,,   68.   ,,
107. Prescott, Huyton, &c   ,,   68   ,,
108. St. Helen's, Burton Wood   ,,   67.   ,,
109. Warwick, &c   6s
111. Cheadale, part of Stockport, &c.
112. Stockport, &c   4s.
113. Part of Liverpool &c.   4s
Sheets 84, 85, 92, 93, 104, and 101 are included in the one-inch Map 89 SW and are described in the "Memoir of the Geology of the Country around Wigan." Second edition
Price 1s

Lancashire—cont
Sheets 86, 87, 88 (in part), 94, 95, 96 (in part), 102, 103, 104 (in part), are included in the one-inch Map 89 SE., and are described in the "Memoir on the Geology of the Country around Bolton-le-Moors"
Sheets 107, 108, are included in the one-inch Map 80 NW., and are described in the "Memoir on the Geology of the Country round Prescott"
Sheets 88, 89, 96, 97, 104, 105, 111, 112, on the six-inch scale, are included in 89 SW, and are described in a Memoir on the Geology of the Country around Oldham, including Manchester and its Suburbs.

Durham
Scale, six inches to a mile

Sheet.		
1 Ryton 4s.	10. Edmond Byers 4s
2 Gateshead 4s.	11 Ebchester.
3. Jarrow. 4s.	13 Chester-le-Street. 6s.
4. S. Shields. 4s.	14 Chester-le-Street.
5 Greenside. 4s.	17 Waskerley.
6 Winlaton	19 Lanchester. 6s. Vertical Section, 39.
7. Washington.	20. Hetton-le-Hole.
8 Sunderland.	25. Wolsingham
9 —— 4s.	26 Brancepeth.

Northumberland.
Scale, six inches to a mile.

47. Coquet Island 4s	84 Newborough.
56. Druridge Bay, &c.	85. Chollerton.
65. Newbiggin 4s.	86 Matfen
68 Belingham	87. Heddon-on-the-Wall.
69 Redesdale.	88 Long Benton.
72 Bedlington	89 Tynemouth
73 Blyth. 4s	95. Corbridge.
77. Swinburn	96 Horsley 4s.
78. Ingoe 6s	97 Newcastle-on-Tyne. 4s.
80. Cramlington.	98 Walker 4s
81. Earsdon.	109. Shotleyfield

These Sheets are included in 105 NE , One inch.

Yorkshire.

261 Bingley	274 Barnsley.
246. Huddersfield.	281 Langsell.
260. Honley	287 Low Bradford.
272 Holmfirth.	293 Hallam Moors. 4s.
273. Penistone

SCOTLAND.
Scale, six inches to a mile

Edinburghshire.

2 Edinburgh, &c	12. Penicuick, Coalfields of Lasswade, &c
3. Portobello, Mussel-burgh, &c.	13 Temple, &c.
6 Gilmerton, Burdie House, &c	14 Pathead. 4s.
7. Dalkeith, &c	17. Brunston Colliery, &c.
8 Preston Hall 4s	18. Howgate

These Sheets are included in Sheet 32, One-inch scale.
8. Preston Hall, &c.   14 Fala, &c

Haddingtonshire.
Six inches to a mile.

8 Prestonpans, &c.   Price 4s
9 Trenent, Gladsmuir, &c.   Price 6s.
13. Elphinstone, &c   Price 4s.
14 Ormiston, East Salton, &c
These Sheets are included in Sheet 32, One-inch scale
Horizontal Sections 92, 63, and Vertical Section 28 illustrate these Six-inch Maps.

Fifeshire.
Six inches to a mile.

24. Markinch, &c.	33 Buckhaven.
25 Scoonie, &c	35 Dunfermline
30. Beath, &c.	36. Kinghorn.
31 Auchterderran 4s	37. Kinghorn 4s
32 Dysart, &c.	

Ayrshire.
Six inches to one mile

19. Newmilns	36 Grieve Hill.
26. Glenbuck. 4s	40. Chiltree.
27. Monkton, &c	41 Dalleagler
28. Tarbolton, &c	42 New Cumnock.
30 Aird's Moss	46. Dalmellington.
31 Muirkirk 4s.	47 Benbeock
33. Ayr, &c.	50 Daily
34. Coylton.	52. Glenmoat.

MINERAL STATISTICS
Embracing the produce of Tin, Copper, Lead, Silver, Zinc, Iron, Coals, and other Minerals By ROBERT HUNT, F R S, *Keeper of Mining Records.* From 1853 to 1857, inclusive, 1s 6d. each. 1858, Part I, 1s 6d ; Part II, 5s   1859, 1s 6d , 1860, 3s. 6d., 1861, 2s., and Appendix, 1s   1862, 2s. 6d   1863, 2s. 6d. 1864, 2s.   1865, 2s 6d   1866 to 1871, &c. each.

THE IRON ORES OF GREAT BRITAIN.
Part I. The IRON ORES of the North and North Midland Counties of England (*Out of print*). Part II. The IRON

CPSIA information can be obtained at www.ICGtesting.com
Printed in the USA
BVOW07s1657240214

345850BV00008B/467/P